MY MOTHER SAID...

A Collection of Quips, Quotes, and Anecdotes

Caroline E. Gardiner

**My Mother Said…: A Collection
of Quips, Quotes, and Anecdotes**
Copyright © 2024 Caroline E. Gardiner

Produced and printed by Stillwater River Publications.

Visit our website at **www.StillwaterPress.com** for more information.

First Stillwater River Publications Edition

ISBN: 978-1-963296-12-9

Library of Congress Control Number: 2024903007

Names: Gardiner, Caroline E., author.
Title: My mother said … : a collection of quips, quotes, and anecdotes /
    Caroline E. Gardiner.
Description: First Stillwater River Publications edition. | West Warwick,
    RI, USA : Stillwater River Publications, [2024]
Identifiers: ISBN: 978-1-963296-12-9 (paperback) | LCCN: 2024903007
Subjects: LCSH: Gardiner, Caroline E.—Family—Anecdotes. | Mothers—
    Anecdotes. | Families—Anecdotes. | Conduct of life—Anecdotes. |
    Resilience (Personality trait)—Anecdotes. | Perseverance (Ethics)—
    Anecdotes. | LCGFT: Anecdotes. | Autobiographies.
Classification: LCC: HQ734 .G37 2024 | DDC: 306.85—dc23

1 2 3 4 5 6 7 8 9 10

Written by Caroline E. Gardiner.
Cover and interior design by Elisha Gillette.
Published by Stillwater River Publications, West Warwick, RI, USA.

This book is simply dedicated to all the mothers out there.
Wear your cape proudly.

"Youth fades; love droops; the leaves of friendship fall;
a mother's secret hope outlives them all."
–Oliver Wendell Holmes

"Motherhood is the exquisite inconvenience of being
another person's everything." *–Unknown*

My mother said…

"Make sure you have clean underwear on in case you
  get into an accident."   *–Judy, 58*

"Six of one, half dozen of the other."   *–Jeff, 50*
                    (when choosing between name brand and store brand)

"I was the strongest woman she ever raised."
                                              –Heidi, 52

"I was seventeen and she set the tone of a conversation by giving me clearance, one hundred percent comfort, and an invitation to come out to her. We had been talking about my brother's girlfriends du jour, then she said, 'So Jeffrey, when do you think you'll bring home a nice girlfriend of yours for me to meet?' To which I replied, 'Mom, I think you know the answer to that, and thank you so much for bringing it up this way.' We pretty much bawled our eyes out for 20 minutes. My sister, Susan, was there too and that conversation and her honest acceptance of me being gay set the stage for the rest of my life and the confidence I needed to be a secure, happy, gay man."

—Jeffrey, 53

"If you want to dance, you've got to pay for the band."

–Jeffrey, 53

"The best revenge is to live a happy life."

–Herb, 66

"Take care of your pennies and your dollars will take care of themselves." *–Herb, 66*

"I am the most handsome Cambodian person and sometimes I am reckless and have no self-control."

–Andrew, 22

"Remember to pick your battles, there's no need to win them all." *–Evelyn, 50*

"Learn the games that people play, then you can decide whether you want to join them or not."

–Elden, 45

"The key to adjusting to new people and places is being more interested and less interesting."

–Elden, 45

"Later in life, when talking to my current girlfriend; 'I would never be able to kick out one of my kids.' Meanwhile, she kicked me out at 17." *—Brett*

"The one thing that sticks with me is the bad life we had because of my father being an abusive alcoholic, and my mother always felt stuck and helpless in never knowing what to do with having had six children with this man. The one thing she would always say to us in the worst of times is, 'Better days are coming.' At that time we never really believed it, but I have learned that nothing ever stays the same and there is always a way out of the darkness. I hold those words close to my heart and have passed them on to my own children because I now truly understand the power of those four little words." *–Dawn, 62*

"Invest in your own happiness, not others."

–Esmeralda, 27

"When we were kids and we were getting out of line, her favorite thing to say to us was, 'I give up with you kids!'"

–Dean, 61

"Don't pluck your eyebrows too thin, because some-day you'll lose eyebrow hair and have to fill them in."

–Denise, 49

"My dad died unexpectedly four weeks prior to my 30th birthday. I had been singing with a band traveling nationally and internationally since the age of 19 and I did not want to continue traveling. At this point, I had lost my spark and was overcome with grief. In discussions about a career and life change, my mom said, "Well, you're not young and pretty anymore so how about using that brain of yours?" *–Diane, 66*

"It must be pretty darn good in Heaven, because no one ever comes back."   *–Betsi*

"Saying thank you never goes out of style."   *–Betsi*

"God wants you to be a friend to the student that's sitting alone and no one wants to be friends with."
–Darlene, 54

"Treat the janitor with the same respect as you would the owner of the building you're entering."
–Darlene, 54

"If you don't have anything nice to say, don't say anything at all!"   *–Bruce, 56*

"If you don't like what I'm cooking then too bad, either eat it or starve."   *–Takiyah, 45*

"I have big shoulders, you can always share anything with me."   *–Mary Lou, 67*

"Never rely on anyone for anything, focus on your education and your career, get your own car/apartment. Don't give anyone the opportunity to say 'if it wasn't for me, you wouldn't have etc.'"   *–Addessa, 25*

"Any number worked for the song *Seventy-Six Trombones.*"   *–Amanda, 34*

"Always show your love no matter what is going on, you may not have a lot of money, but family is what matters."   *–Amanda, 34*

"Less something said, more something done."

–Dave

"We are definitely not in Heaven yet."   *–Chris*

"Nothing good happens after midnight."

–Jenny, 26

"Talk to my head because my ass hurts."

–David, 57

"You play, you pay."   *–Candy, 53*

(Said to my 15-year-old sister in labor)

"Men will go through hell and high water to get to you if they really care for you."   *–Heidi, 57*

"You have to judge people by their insides, not the outside."   *–Heidi, 57*

"*Shweeze na cabesa.*' Portuguese for brains in the head. It was often said when we were headed out for the night. She said it so often that she shortened it to '*Schweeze.*'"   *–Scott, 69*

"After she was diagnosed, she told me she was okay with it. 'I never expected to live forever.'"   *–Scott, 69*

"My mother said to me when I was 15, 'I'm not worried about YOU,' as she was venting over something one of my sisters had done to worry her. I knew she didn't mean it literally but still didn't like the feeling it gave me. I have two older kids now and to this day, I have purposely never said those words to either one. Mom's words had power."   *–Jim, 57*

"It's not a sale if you can't afford it."

–Donna, 62

"When I was six years old, there was a big construction debris fire burning on the beach a quarter mile away. Before going out to play, Mom said, 'Do not go near that fire.' I told her, 'I won't, Mom.' The first thing I do when I leave the house is head straight to the fire to play. My mom sees this and proceeds to beat my ass with every syllable contained in the sentence. 'I told you not to go near that fire!'"   –Rick, 65

"ou make your bed; you lie in it."
–Gail

"My mother never swore, she would always say, 'Jesus, Mary and Joseph.' or, 'I could just spit,' in my family, spitting was not a very ladylike thing to do. I also remember when I was in my twenties; I said to her, 'Mom, you never told me anything about sex.' Her answer, 'You probably know more than I do now.' If she got mad, she would go through all our names—there were six of us—and the dog and cat before she would get to yours. *–Carol*

16

"If a guy says all the right things, it's because he's had a lot of practice."   *–Liz*

"Shari, make sure you take care of your teeth, because if not, you'll end up spitting them out like corn"
                                                                –Shari, 63

And of course, now I have thousands invested in them.

"Remember, you'll never find happiness through someone else's tears."   *–Debbie*

"Although we didn't have much, we wanted for nothing."   *–Gian, 57*

"Always be kind."   *–Gian, 57*

"Keep your sunny side up."   *–Sarah, 42*

"Someday you're going to have a kid just like you."
                                                              –Barbara, 57

"There were eight of us kids so of course my mother had a handful to watch. Whenever we were acting crazy or did something wrong, my mother would say, 'Wait till your father gets home!' It wasn't like my father was overly mean or beat us, but he had, at an early age, instilled in each and every one of us that he was in charge, so when my mother said that—and it wasn't like she used it all the time—we knew we were in trouble!"

–Bob, 70

"If you want to get out of a hole, quit digging."

–Jeff, 54

"Go play in traffic…heavy traffic."   *–Tim, 57*

"Nothing good happens after 2 am."   *–Autumn, 35*

"Drive safe and text me when you're there, love you."

–Danielle, 28

"My mother is like me and repeats herself, and 'til this day she will say, 'Always want more.' When I was down, she said, 'I am your biggest cheerleader,' and lastly, 'I will always be your momma first.'"

–Harrison, 28

"Say what you mean, mean what you say."

–Marc, 53

"Hate is a very strong word, never use the word hate, you don't hate anyone."   *–Marc, 53*

"Don't be afraid of the dead, they can't hurt you, it's the living you have to watch out for!"   *–Marc, 53*

"If my mother dressed me in something I didn't like and I complained, she would say, 'What makes you think you're so important that anybody cares?'"

–Diane, 73

"I brought you in this world and I'll take you out."

–Leo, 61

"Love is blind, but marriage is an eye opener."

–Leo, 61

"This too shall pass."   *–Brooke, 12*

"Thank you, God, for the sunny day!"   *–Angie, 42*

"Laughing leads to crying."   *–Karen, 57*

"Everything will be different in seven days, just give it seven days."   *–Colleen, 51*

"Never depend on a man. Have your own money and career."   *–Marcelina, 15*

"Read books so you can be a good speller."
–Ava, 13

"Enjoy being a kid while you can because you're an adult longer than you have a childhood."
–Marcelina, 15

"Speak your mind." *–Ava, 13*

"I can't hear you, I don't have my eyes in."
–Harrison, 28

"When someone shows you who they are, believe them." *–Teagan, 26*

"Everyone's got something going on, everyone's got a bag of shit." *–Teagan, 26*

"Live like no one is watching." *–Nicky, 24*

"My mom is superstitious…if bread fell on the floor, we had to kiss it before throwing it away with the sign of the cross. If I looked up in the sky at night, she would say, 'Don't point at the stars or count them because you'll get warts.' She would kiss us before bed goodnight and good morning, even if she was angry with us. Tuesdays and Fridays were not good days to clip our nails or cut our hair or buy a car or house or travel, if we had a headache, she would make the cross on our foreheads against evil eyes of envious people. For example, someone during the day would give us a compliment and say how pretty I was but didn't mean it, they are called 'Malocchio', evil eyes. She would get a bowl with water and sea salt grains and drop oil in the dish, if the drop of oil spread, we had the evil eye, if the oil kept its shape, we were okay."

–Carla, 58

"Sit like a lady and keep your legs closed!"

–Liz, 65

"I can honestly say that when I look in the mirror, I am content with myself. I don't see ugly or fat or insignificant and I cannot remember a time when I felt genuinely bad about myself. I have long since realized this is because of my mom. However, she didn't accomplish this with the things she said, rather, what she *didn't* say. My mom never told me I needed a husband. So, I wasn't disappointed in myself when I chose not to marry.

My mom never told me to wear makeup or lose weight. So, I never felt like I needed to change into something I'm not. My mom never told me I couldn't do something. So, there was nothing I felt was out of reach for me. My mom supported me even when she silently disagreed. So, I was confident in my decisions. My mom never, ever told me I wasn't enough. So, I am. My mother sacrificed a great deal of her life giving to others. I recognize the good parts of me come from her and am grateful. I hope to be just like her when I grow up..."

–Colleen, 53

"I never wanted a daughter; I only wanted a son."

–Tara, 46

"I know you are not going to keep the baby, you need to get rid of it." *–Tara, 46*

"It's never the wrong time or wrong place to do the right thing." *–Doug, 64*

"You'll never have luck with stolen property."

–Rebecca, 43

"One day you will have a daughter just like you."

–Rebecca, 43

"If you change the way you think, you change the way you feel."   *–Anthony, 22*

"Can you see? I bet there are many people that can't see that would trade with you. Can you walk? I bet a person that is in a wheelchair would love to be able to run like you can. Can you hear? What would someone that can't hear music or the birds sing trade for your hearing?"   *–Jane, 71*

"The world is so full of a number of things; I think we should all be as happy as kings."   *–Sheila, 61*

"Just breathe."   *–Sheila, 61*

"My mother never raised her voice and never (overtly anyway) criticized. Growing up and as a young adult, I did not get along with my mother and disparaged her. Once I was a mother myself, I recognized what a feat it was for her to be so patient and uncritical and came to appreciate and try to emulate—though I remain far from achieving that standard myself!"   *–Pat, 76*

"Go take a shower, you will feel better!"

–Lauren, 34

"Never change plans for a better offer! Once you commit to something, keep that commitment, and don't cancel because you can do something better."

–Paula, 65

"During the market crash of 08, I was in fear of losing everything. Mom was self-employed for over thirty years, and I asked her advice on what to do. Her reply, 'Trim overhead and payroll, lace up your boots and work harder than you've ever worked in your life, you'll weather the storm.'"

–Jerry, 58

"Every time I did something bad or wrong, 'God will punish you for that.' As she brushed my hair, 'It hurts to be beautiful.'" *–Amanda, 42*

"Brush your teeth and say your prayers, never go to bed angry." *–CO*

"If you don't brush your teeth, you will never be kissed by a boy." *–Amanda, 42*

"A beautiful girl can wear a trash bag and still be beautiful." *–Amanda, 42*

"Don't play leapfrog with a unicorn."   *–Dave, 48*

"I love you, but that doesn't mean I like you."
                                            –Stacey, 35

"You're killing me."   *–Kerri, 35*

"My mother says, 'Fuck'…a lot."   *–Khalen, 16*

"Be fifteen minutes early to any appointment, always follow through with anything you start, always pay your bills early just in case, and make sure you have clean underwear on because you never know what could happen." *–Aimee, 56*

"When I told my mom I wanted to quit cheerleading, she told me, 'You are part of the team, and you cannot!' Also, one time, I got mad and stood on the front porch and said I was going to live with my dad, and she said, 'Be my guest!' I was a horrible child—really, who could handle five children—but now here I am taking care of her." *–Lori, 57*

"My mom was always prim and proper, and her own mother referred to her as 'The original Puritan' but in 1949, she used a glamour picture to 'trap' my father, who was a WW2 veteran, to return to Worcester when he finished school in Pennsylvania…it worked!"

–Barry, 61

"When my mom had a stroke, I quit my job as a tenured professor at Western Carolina University to be back with her and as a result, I really needed work and all I could grab was a gig at Community Care Van as a driver. One day, I was assigned to the route my mom was on, to the adult day care center and with permission from the rider's caregivers, I took them all out for a treat of ice cream at Frates Drive In on route 138 in Taunton. We spent a few minutes at the duck pond on Somerset Avenue on the way down to Frates. It brought back so many memories in each of these folks. Listening to their stories of their younger years was such a joy. This was a top-secret operation but the next day my boss got a call from the daycare director trying to get me into trouble. My boss was quite understanding and said, 'Do it, but don't get caught next time.' My mom was pretty happy she witnessed a breaking of the rules that day." —*Paul, 69*

"Don't be a nudnik."   *–Matt, 50*

"If you keep eating those, pretty soon you'll turn into a chicken nugget."   *–Brooke, 27*

"Keep crying and I'll give you something to cry about."   *–Lisa, 62*

"Be home when the streetlights come on."

–Lisa, 62

"Don't go outside with wet hair, you're going to get sick."   *–Piero, 47*

"You'll never know until you have kids of your own."

–Betty, 50

"To each his own."   *–Nancy, 60*

"Clean your plate; waste not, want not."   *–Kevin*

"Eat your corn, money doesn't grow on trees."

–Steve, 72

"God is good, but it's too bad we have to die and leave others to mourn." *—Julie, 57*

"I know now life is too short, get out there and enjoy it." *—Julie, 57*

"If I could go back, I'd go on more vacations with all of you." *—Julie, 57*

"All you can do is try your best." *—Elizabeth, 40*

"Meglio essere quello gentile che l'unico gentile." *—Aldo*
(better to be the kind one than the only kind)

"Always do your homework and no more than four cookies at any given time." *—Daniel*

"It is my job as a mother to worry." *—Chanly, 42*

"Friends come and go but family is forever." *—Madeline, 85*

"To anyone who would listen, 'My daughter is a great cook; she cooks just like me!'" *—Madeline, 85*

"Have more confidence in yourself."   *–Linda, 68*

"Everyone needs a full-length mirror."   *–Janet*

"If you can help someone, do it, you'll need help someday."   *–Kathleen*

"If you do things in order in life, life is easier."
–Kathleen

"Eat your vegetables, dessert comes when the plate is clear."   *–CO*

"Always have enough money to get yourself home."
–Kathleen

"No one will love you like your mother."
–Caroline, 57

"Believe in yourself!"   *–Jill, 57*

"I have three siblings so there was a lot of, 'Mom, Mom, Mom!' She used to say, 'I'm going to change my name to Gertrude!' We'd ask her what's for dinner and we'd get, 'Shit on a shingle'. 'If you don't have anything nice to say, don't say it at all' was also a big one. 'Go ask your father' because she knew we wouldn't and the one thing I still say that she used to say is, 'I love you, heart and soul.' I can still hear her say that."

–Jeniene, 57

"Women are born without balls because they are already broken before they are even born."

–Erica, 28

"My mom would tuck me into bed and say, 'I love you with all my heart, high as the sky, deep as the sea, you're my baby.'" *–Tanisha, 36*

"Don't bite your nose to spite your face."

–Donald, 78

"Always overtip breakfast waitresses."

–Amanda, 28

"Do everything by yourself and be independent, do not expect to rely on others." *–Fred*

"If you don't die, you get old." *–Fred*

"I hope you have kids that do just half of what you've done to me…just half!" *–Joe, 60*

"Always make sure you have a twenty-dollar bill stashed in your purse for an emergency when you go out." *–Paula, 65*

(of course there were no ATMs or cell phones, so we needed that emergency cash)

"You never know what someone is going through, be kind." *–Amanda, 28*

"You will be able to do anything that you need and want, you have the skills that no one else has. Look for ways to provide service and we will be happy and from there, you will be rich." *–Nick, 39*

"Paddle your own canoe." *–Jon, 60*

"I'll wipe that smirk off your face." *–Karen, 54*

"It is what it is so sit back and breathe, tomorrow is a new day." *–CK, 24*

"The love for your mother is always within you. What happens when there is cruelty that surrounds your environment; the love for your mother is still in your heart. Throughout my life, I have gone through a lot of being slapped and cursed out regularly. I had to live with relatives in a different state for seven years because my mother was a murderer, and yet, the love for my mother was still there. Going back to my mother after seven years was very hard for me. She was an alcoholic but the love for my mother was still there. Many years later, as I became an adult, my mother stopped drinking and began to mother her children. It is never too late to show your kids love because their love for their mother is always there."   *–Adele, 70*

"Some days are just sweatpants days."

–Michael, 42

"Do onto others as you would want done to yourself."

–CO

"I want to go to the moon, but I don't have a ladder."

–Marina, 34

"Just because I don't say it doesn't mean I don't know what's going on."   *–Caroline, 57*

"Go to sleep and leave it to God."   *–Marina, 34*

"Never be afraid to ask questions, the worst they can say is no!"   *–Amanda, 42*

"You can't un-ring the bell."   *–Caroline, 57*

"The older I get, the less I know."   *–Caroline, 57.*

"You live or you die because you're supposed to."

–Caroline, 57

"Second best won't do." *–Jon, 58*

"Only those that are willing to risk going too far will ever truly know how far they can go."

–Jon, 58

"Go safely, come back safely, and in the middle have a wonderful time." *–Bob, 57*

"A handful of gimme and a mouthful of much obliged."

"Every time your elbow bends, your mouth flies open."

"All shut eyes ain't sleep and goodnights ain't gone."

"Eavesdroppers don't hear nothing good."

"Play with puppies, they lick your mouth, play with the big dogs and they'll bite you."

–Toni, 57

"It's not what you say, it's how you say it."

–Josh, 29

"You leave the house as one person, you come back one person." *–Tammara, 33*

"Never depend on a man for anything."

–Tiffany, 42

"Fix your face or hide your face because people are always looking at you." *–Cindia*

"If you drop a fork, a strange man will come to your house." *–Tiffany, 42*

"Someone can tell you to leave a situation over and over again, but you won't until YOU are ready. You will wake up one day and realize that you need to leave the situation." *–Cindia*

"It is bad luck to not have salt in your house."

–Tiffany, 42

"Always move in silence. You will never know who hates you and will not want you to succeed in life."

–Cindia

"Never take a man back after a failed relationship; if it didn't work out the first time, it will not work out the next time."

–Tiffany, 42

"Love yourself first before loving a man."   *–Cindia*

"If you lie, your nose will grow."   *–CO*

"Before you get with a man, look at his life. If he has children, pay attention to how he treats them and how he treats the mother of his children because this will determine if you are able to live your life with him."

–Cindia

"Trust no one with your children because it will be the ones who you trust that hurt them."   *–Cindia*

"Everybody is not your friend." *–Cindia*

"You get more with honey than you do with vinegar."
–CO

"Never wear dirty underwear or socks because it may be your last day on earth." *–Cindia*

"There is always a reason why people come to our path, either you need them at the moment to change your life or you may be the one that will change their life." *–Cindia*

"Treat others the way you would want to be treated."
–Kevin, 63

48

"My dad passed away in February 1982 when I was 11. That summer, I played my second year of little league, and my mom took my father's place behind the fence watching every one of my games. When our team had its annual Father/Son game, I asked my mom if she would just drop me off and she said, 'No, I'm playing unless you're too embarrassed to have your mom out there?' I was pretty excited, actually, but I asked her, 'What if they won't let you play?' And my mother said to me, 'I'd like to see them stop me!' She played and I was proud! I will never forget that day or what she did for me. On another note, she told me that if I kept playing with my belly button, my bum would fall down, and that I'd get worms if I ate cake frosting out of the container!"

–*Todd, 53*

"You're going to be sorry someday."   *–Beth, 63*

"Make hay while the sun shines today, you can do it.
God forbid tomorrow you might not be able to do
it, or the work might not be there."   *–Tom*

"Well, to be transparent, my mom and I didn't have the best relationship growing up and it's still improving day by day. We both struggle with mental health issues that make it hard for us to see eye to eye most of the time. But we always make sure no matter where we are and no matter what happens each day, we always say "Good night, I love you" each night because my mother says, "I could die in my sleep, God forbid, so you never go to bed angry."

–Breonna, 28

"My mother was the general of eight kids and if she didn't get her way, you got dad's size 12 boot in your ass!" *–Kevin*

"When I transferred to St. Leo College (now University) her words of wisdom went like this, 'We aren't' sending you to Florida to find a wife but to get an education!' I believe it was her last-ditch effort trying to get me to be a priest! I ended up doing both; got a degree and wife while avoiding becoming a man of the cloth!"

–Allen, 60

"Your mouth is going to get you in trouble one day."
                                                    –CO

"Always dress to impress because it can be your last
day on earth."   *–Cindia*

"If you're born round, you can't die square."
                                         –Marina, 34

"Why would a boy buy the cow if he can get the milk
for free."   *–CO*

"To be early is to be on time, to be on time is to be late."
                                                    –CO

"It takes a bigger person to admit when they are wrong, if you make a mistake, learn from it."

–CO

"They're the boss and you're the horse."

–Caroline, 57

"There is always room for one more."   *–CO*

"My mother was a nurse so if I called home with cramps, she'd tell the nurse to send me back and would ask, 'Is it math or science you're trying to get out of?'"   *–CO*

"Whenever I brought a girl home and asked my mother what she thought, my mother—who never spoke poorly of anyone—would simply say, 'What ever happened to Sarah?'"

—Francis, 62

"I asked my mother, 'How will I know if she's the right one to marry?' Her reply, 'It's not finding someone you can live with; it's finding someone you can't live without.'"

—Francis, 62

"Don't judge anyone too quickly, you don't know the fight they've had to deal with. Be tolerant and kind and try to understand the person; no one is mean for no reason."   *–Lou, 33*

"Wait until your dad gets home."

"Money doesn't grow on trees."

"I'll wash your mouth out with soap."

"Children should be seen, not heard."

"This will hurt me more than it will hurt you."
                                                  –Milt, 72

"Keep on keeping on."   *–Mark*

"My mother used to tell me all the time, 'Go to college because you will never make any money farming.' All I ever wanted was to be a farmer and she was so against it. And forty-eight years later, I'm farming. Maybe not making lots of money but doing what I love, and it's funny because now she is my biggest supporter!"

–Erin

"You're going to be a loser, just like your father."

—Eric, 47

"Call me as soon as you get there!!!' When I was younger, we used to ride our bikes from my house to my best friend's house and vice versa and when we would ride our bikes, we would sing this song, 'Call mom, ca-ca-ca-ca-ca-call mom, call mom, ca-ca-ca-ca-call mom" in order so we would not forget to call our mothers when we would arrive at the friend's house to let her know that we were there safely." *–Laura, 38*

"Ignore the ignorant."   –*Peggy, 67*

"Growing up it was just me and my mother. Just us, and I watched my mother work a lot to make ends meet to always make sure I lived a 'normal life.' So whenever I feel like life is just tumbling around me, or I have this dark cloud above me, I always remember her telling me, 'we don't back down, we keep the faith and move forward, we are strong' and 'As long as we're doing our best, that's all she cares about,' but most importantly she always said, 'Keep that smile on that beautiful face of yours, Mama is always proud of you!'" *–Monica, 27*

"My mom would always tell me to 'Look at people with my heart open and my eyes closed,' then she would say that 'most people don't need the judgements, expectations, or opinions we place on them, everyone has weight to carry and we shouldn't add to that weight but help them carry it if we can.'" *–John, 50*

"I'll smash you."   *–Chris, 56*

"You need to give it all up to God. Jesus has died for
    your sins."   *–Chris, 56*

"You are the devil, a cancerous growth."   *–Dick, 61*

"Oh, what a wicked web we weave when first we set
    out to deceive."   *–Tiffany, 47*

"I'll always be honest with you even if that makes
    me the bad guy. I'll be the bad guy and you can be
    mad at me, but I'll tell you the truth and not what
    you want to hear."   *–April*

"I hope your kids turn out like you."   *–Brian*

"Follow your dreams, follow your heart, God, and
    your gut. Fall in love with someone's heart. Don't
    hurry love. Appreciate what you have."   *–Ken*

"A laugh before a cry."   *–Jenny, 26*

"There's three rules: Never talk religion, never talk
    politics, and never sleep with a married man."

                                               –Janine, 57

"Ever since we've had our cell phones, my mother ends the conversation with, 'Okay, bye I love you, mwah,' and blows kisses. This can be five times a day. —*Teagan 26*

ABOUT THE AUTHOR

CAROLINE GARDINER is a Moon child, Momma bear, Veteran, Life-Cycle Celebrant/Wedding Officiant, daydreamer, and lover of Love. She lives in Southeastern Massachusetts with a couple of crazy cats, Bonnabelle and Pistachio.